Survive Bullying
at Work

How to stand up for yourself and
take control

Lorenza Clifford

A & C Black • London

First published in 2006 by
A & C Black Publishers Ltd.
38 Soho Square
London W10 3HB

British Library Cataloguing in Publication Data
A CIP record for this book is available from the British Library.

A & C Black uses paper produced with elemental chlorine-free pulp,
harvested from managed sustainable forests.

ISBN-10: 0-7136-7520-9
ISBN-13: 978-0-7136-7520-7

Design by Fiona Pike, Pike Design, Winchester
Typeset by RefineCatch Limited, Bungay, Suffolk
Printed in Italy by Legoprint

Contents

About the author

Lorenza Clifford is founder of **Coachange Ltd**,
a company that provides top quality coaching to individuals.

Career coaching helps people to find better balance in their
lives, to make their work enlivening and their leisure time
happier. We prepare our clients to rise to life's challenges
and to make the most of every opportunity.

Coachange Ltd works with clients from all walks of life
finding new ways to make quality coaching affordable. We
believe coaching can offer powerful help to ordinary people,
not just the elite.

Lorenza has a Masters degree in Occupational Psychology,
a coaching qualification and over a decade of experience
coaching blue chip clients at all levels of the organisation.

She is a member of the Association for Coaching and is
available for workshops, coaching, speaking and writing.
To contact her, e-mail headoffice@coachange.co.uk or
telephone 01264 334897.

Visit Lorenza's website at: **www.coachange.co.uk**

Thanks

My thanks go to Dr Sandi Mann for introducing the concept
of emotional work when we first worked together on MERI™
surveys many moons ago. Thanks also to my editor, Lisa
Carden, and my family for all their support.

Are you being bullied?

We all have a mental image of the playground bully, but that type of damaging behaviour can continue through to other parts of our lives. Bullying is, sadly, very much a part of working life for some people. Take the following quiz to assess your preconceptions of the office bully, and judge how well you and your colleagues are dealing with this common problem.

1. How widespread do you think workplace bullying is?

2. Which of the following would you perceive to be symptomatic that a friend or colleague is being bullied?

   - Crying
   - Being over-emotional
   - Behaving irrationally
   - Loss of self-confidence
   - Changes in sleeping and eating patterns
   - Clumsiness
   - Loss of libido
   - Excessive drinking
   - Stress
   - Ill-health

3. Can you tell the difference between constructive criticism and bullying?

4. What is your impression of a stereotypical bully?

5. Why do you think a person gets bullied?

6. Is 'doing nothing' ever an option?

7. What is the best way out?

Answers

1. Remarkably few work-places can consider themselves to be "bully-free". In 2005, the TUC estimated that 18 million working days are lost every year in the United Kingdom as a result of bullying.
2. All of these changes in a person can be symptomatic of being bullied. Work, social and private lives can be severely affected, and the levels of anxiety and stress caused can be seriously derogatory to your mental and physical health. If you think someone you know is a victim of bullying, or recognise these factors in yourself, then please do get help. This book contains much practical advice and support, so read on.
3. No one likes to be criticised, but it's important to look at a situation objectively, and ask yourself if the criticism you receive is truly unfair, or harshly given in such a way that causes offence or embarrassment. Turn to Chapter 1 for more advice on this issue.

4. Some bullies are socially inept, some show sociopathic tendencies, while others manipulate and insinuate to increase their power and status. Others still pass on the overwork and aggression they get from others on to you. Chapter 2 looks in details at the different types of office bully, how to spot them, and how to handle them.

5. In truth, people are bullied for a wide array of reasons. Bullying can because of gender, age or ethnicity — or seemingly at random — and is no less likely to occur at the top of an organisation than it is lower down. Whatever the reason, it's just not acceptable. Chapter 3 will help you identify the triggers for bullying, and understand why and how bullying cycles start.

6. Sometimes, yes. If the bullying persists or escalates, however, you must act. If you're being bullied yourself, you need to protect your own wellbeing. If you are an employer, you also have a duty of care towards your employees. If you are working in organisation where individuals or the system seems to be attacking another individual, you may even consider blowing the whistle on the bullies. Turn to Chapter 7 for advice on taking this step.

7. The best way out depends very much on you or your situation. If you feel that moving on and finding a new job. Chapter 5 can help you with this route. Alternatively, Chapter 6 can help if you decide to stay and fight. Good luck!

What is bullying?

Conflict happens at work, as in all areas of human interaction. It is a normal, if unpleasant, part of working life.

Some people might argue that a little conflict is healthy now and again—that a frank exchange of views can work to improve communication and understanding of perspectives or it can be a catalyst for change. But when conflict and domination become a habit or are constantly created or sought, they harm the target(s) and make the work environment toxic, this is bullying.

As bullying at work becomes a more common problem, research has been conducted on it by a variety of organisations all around the world. The International Labour Organization has defined it as:

'offensive behaviour through vindictive, cruel, malicious or humiliating attempts to undermine an individual or groups of employees'

Bullying:

■ is behaving in a way perceived by others as negative

- ■ is perceived to be done with the intent to do harm
- ■ is repeated and persistent, often becoming worse with time
- ■ may be directed at one or many people
- ■ may be carried out by one or many people
- ■ happens where there is an imbalance of power between the bully and the target, making it difficult for the target to defend him/herself

This book is designed to help you if you are being bullied yourself, or if you are a manager concerned about members of your staff. The first two chapters will look at what bullying is, what makes bullies behave as they do, and why they focus on some people rather than others. It will then move on to look at how to cope with bullying at work—there *are* options open to you and people who can help.

Step one: Understand you're not alone

Recent research into bullying has revealed that it is widespread. Bullies are present in all sectors of work and in all types of organisation. In some sectors bullying seems to be more frequent, even an expected part of the working culture. There are very few workplaces that can consider themselves bully-free. From the top of the organisation to

front line workers, your place in the hierarchy does not
protect you from the bullies.

If you are reading this because you are being bullied, you're
not alone. In November 2005, the Trades Union Congress
(TUC) estimated that 18 million working days a year were lost
in the United Kingdom as the result of bullying. In a survey
conducted by the TUC, more than two million people
claimed to have been bullied at work in the previous six
months.

Bearing these startling figures in mind, it's likely that at some
stage in your career you'll come into contact with cases of
bullying. Knowing how to protect yourself and others is
important.

Step two: Understand the effects of bullying

Bullying has been shown to have very negative effects on the
health of victims: it's recognised as an extreme form of social
stress. The effects may vary from person to person, but
targets may show a range of symptoms, both psychological
and physical.

If you are bullied you may soon notice that you:

- become over-emotional or easily lose control over your
  emotions

- have lower resilience than usual, and take longer to bounce back
- suffer from low self-esteem
- blame yourself when others criticise you
- find it hard to switch off, and sleep less well, perhaps having nightmares
- lose your sense of humour
- make mistakes or become less reliable at work
- lose your self-confidence

TOP TIP
In UK law employees have a 'duty of care' towards their colleagues in the workplace. Health and Safety regulations require employers to take steps against all threats to employee health and this includes bullying. Organisations need to have an anti-bullying policy and should make sure that their employees are aware of how to recognise bullying and protect against it.

Step three: Recognise bullying

If you are targeted by a bully, it may be some time before you realise what is actually happening. Bullying often starts with relatively trivial events that escalate into a pattern of violence or intimidation, eventually resulting in psychological damage to the victim(s) as well as physical illness. Because the onset of bullying is gradual, many targets do not take action early enough and by the time they do seek help, they're often suffering extreme physical symptoms and may require a long period of recuperation to recover.

As well as hearing reports of or witnessing bullying events, spouses, partners, friends, and colleagues of targets may notice some of the following behaviours, all of which can indicate bullying:

- crying
- anxiety
- nervousness
- shortened attention span
- ill health
- changes in sleeping, eating, and working patterns
- loss of libido
- becoming obsessive about things
- memory lapses
- clumsiness
- withdrawal
- excessive focus on work or co-workers
- exhaustion
- drinking alcohol more than usual
- happier on days off but becoming edgy the night before going back to work

If someone you know is in this kind of state and you think it may be due to bullying, take action to help them— targets may not be able to help themselves. Start by gently telling them what you have noticed and that this worries you. Ask them if they can tell you what the matter is.

Step four: Identify bullying in your organisation

Managers and HR staff within an organisation can use both formal monitoring routes and the 'grapevine' to help them identify bullying problems.

Formal indicators of bullying include:

- **formal complaints.** Any formal complaints about bullying should be taken extremely seriously. Ignoring reports of bullying actively encourages bullies to continue their unacceptable behaviour, so take action as soon as possible.
- **sick leave.** If one part of the organisation is experiencing higher rates of sick leave than others, it can be an indicator of a bullying problem. Interestingly, witnesses as well as the targets of bullying are likely to take time off sick. It seems that bullying gives the workplace a nasty atmosphere that employees want to avoid. It may be that witnesses are afraid that they will be the next target of bullying.
- **high exit rates.** If staff are leaving one part of the organisation in droves, there could be a bully at work. This can be hard to see in industries where staff turnover is ordinarily high—in call centres or in the

hospitality industry, for example—but in some more traditional environments, this indicator remains useful.

■ **staff survey results.** If your business has ever conducted staff surveys, look at the results carefully to see if you can identify pockets of low morale. Depending on the wording of the questionnaire, you may be able to identify where to turn your attention to find the bullies in your organisation. Targets and witnesses of bullying are likely to report that they don't enjoy their work, that they are thinking of leaving and that the organisation does not look after its employees. Other areas of response may relate to poor communication and stress. Take these types of response seriously and investigate them thoroughly.

To pick up on informal indicators of bullying:

■ **talk unofficially with staff.** Simply chatting with different people around the workplace can be very beneficial to gauge the level of morale. If you think people are unhappy at work, ask them what you can do to make work a better place for them. They may be looking for an opportunity to get help but not know how or where to begin. Making it easy for people to talk to you allows them the option mentioning workplace problems.

■ **listen to visiting local staff association/union reps or occupational health workers.** Staff association and union reps are often the first people to hear a grievance and may be involved if a formal complaint is to be made. If you want the chance to tackle bullies discreetly, you will need to have open channels. Occupational health workers will not be in a position to divulge confidential information but may be able to use the grapevine to help targets.

Making a stand

If you see anyone persistently doing any of the following, don't just hope for the best—do something. See Chapter 8 for information on whistleblowing:

- subjecting others to unwanted sexual attention or physical attacks
- shouting at people or flying off the handle
- withholding information which affects others' performance
- ignoring the opinions and views of others
- exposing others to unmanageable workloads
- giving people tasks with unreasonable or impossible targets or deadlines
- making insulting or offensive remarks, messages, calls, or e-mails
- humiliating or ridiculing others
- spreading gossip about others
- ordering others to do work that is well below their competence while removing more suitable work from them

Step five: Work out if *you* are being bullied

If you're not sure whether you're being bullied or whether you're just under pressure at work or perhaps being over-sensitive, use this checklist to help you decide what your next step should be.

- When I make a positive contribution it is always ignored or belittled.
- Minor problems or mistakes are blown up and given undue importance.
- My workload keeps increasing.
- I'm given less control over my work.
- My work is being scrutinised and my performance criticised constantly.
- I am not invited to meetings that concern me and my work.
- I never get important information that I need.
- Disciplinary and grievance procedures and warnings are used against me unfairly.
- Information that I ask for is withheld from me without proper reasons offered.
- If a joke or sarcastic comment is made, it is usually at my expense.

If you agree with *most of* the statements above, you may have been targeted by a bully. Seek help.

If you have disagreed with *most of* the statements it is unlikely that you are being bullied.

If you are still doubtful, seeking personal advice or coaching could help.

Common mistakes

✗ You mistake feedback for bullying

In the course of our work we all make mistakes or — mostly inadvertently — do things in a way that is unhelpful to others. Our managers will sometimes need to point out what is happening and ask for a change in our behaviour to iron out these problems. Feedback that is well handled and used to focus your attention on areas where you can develop and improve is known as 'constructive criticism'. Done well, this type of feedback can build a healthy and effective working environment.

Sadly, well-meant feedback is sometimes given clumsily. In the heat of the moment, this can be hurtful. If feedback of this nature is constant, it can be difficult to know if it is simply poor management or active bullying.

If you're trying to work out whether you're experiencing bullying or gauche management, ask yourself:

- Is the person trying to sort things out?
- Are comments focused on important issues?

- Is the feedback useful in some way?
- Are the comments true and reasonably accurate, even if they come from a different perspective?
- Does the criticism relate to realistic standards or tasks?
- Is the person willing to clarify and give examples?
- Is the 'feedback' delivered appropriately? For example, is it given calmly and in an appropriate venue, or is it barked at you in front of others?

If you have answered 'no' to these questions, it's likely that you are being bullied. Don't allow it to continue: Chapter 4 will help you to think about the options available to you.

If you have answered 'yes' to these questions, it may be helpful to discuss with your manager the way that feedback is given, at the same time as trying to clarify what *you* need to do differently.

✗ You don't allow for context

The culture of your workplace and industry has an effect on what behaviours will be considered 'bullying' and which are considered appropriate. For example, in uniformed services and in particular in the Forces, it's reasonable to expect that orders may be shouted; if that happened in a more traditional office setting, however, it would be cause for concern. If you're new to an organisation or its culture, try to find out more about it informally before you make a formal complaint.

STEPS TO SUCCESS

✓ Understand that bullying is not the same as conflict: it is the persistent, malicious use of power to cause hurt and humiliation to targets. Sadly, bullying doesn't stop at the school gate: it is widespread in organisations all over the world.

✓ Don't feel that bullying is something that can be brushed off easily: it can threaten the mental and physical well-being of targets as well as witnesses. In extreme cases, it can result in victims suffering from post-traumatic stress disorder.

✓ Remember that UK Health and Safety law obliges organisations to protect their employees against all threats to health, including bullying.

✓ Realise that bullying is contextual: behaviours that may be seen as completely inappropriate or unreasonable in one context may be considered normal in a different environment.

Useful links

Andrea Adams Trust:
www.andreaadamstrust.org
Bully Online:
www.bullyonline.org

Bullying Institute:

www.bullyinginstitute.org

Dignity at Work:

www.dignityatwork.org

Just Fight On:

www.jfo.org.uk

Trades Union Congress (TUC):

www.tuc.org.uk

Suzy Lamplugh Trust:

www.suzylamplugh.org.uk

Trades Union Congress:

www.tuc.org.uk

Understanding why bullies behave as they do

When you realise you are the target of a bully, probably the last thing in your mind is understanding the person who is persecuting you. However, there are some very important practical points which come from getting a better understanding of why bullying happens. These points may help you to make better decisions about tackling your situation.

Step one: Understand the role of intention

Intention is a key part of any definition of bullying. Bullies are people who repeatedly cause negative reactions in the targets of their behaviour, where the target believes they intend to do them harm. To put it another way, the victim believes that the bully is upsetting them or harming them on purpose.

Despite this, it is possible for bullying to be unintentional. It is the target's view of intention that plays a role in defining bullying. In other words, if the victim *believes* that they are being harmed deliberately through persistently upsetting behaviour or violence, then they are being bullied, regardless of whether there was any *actual* harmful intention on the part of the bully.

Step two: Know your bully

Understanding the types of bullies and the motives involved may help individuals to manage their own situation better. While they may not allow you to predict or prevent bullying in the first place, it may at least mean that you can choose the right course of action as a response.

I Sociopathic or psychopathic bullies

Whilst a victim or a witness may suggest that the bully's behaviour is psychopathic or sociopathic, it is really very unlikely that this is the case. They make up only about 0.5% of the population, with an even lower percentage in the workplace, according to Christopher Matthew in the *Daily Mail*. The American Psychiatric Association has found that approximately 4% of bullies have genuinely disordered personalities.

Psychopaths are totally disconnected from the real world and act purely to satisfy their own internal needs. They lack the inhibitions of self-imposed scruples or morals or externally imposed social norms. They have formed their own unique perspective on the world and how it works and will behave in a way that proves their view to be correct. In an organisation that is unlucky enough to employ this type of

bully, the damage may be considerable because of the
bully's lack of boundaries or conscience.

2 'Self-boosting' bullies

These individuals feel threatened and use bullying behaviour
to boost their self-esteem. They over-rate themselves and
when reality is at odds with their positive views of
themselves, they may get aggressive rather than accept a
less positive self-view. Wounded pride, disrespect, insults,
verbal abuse, or threats to their status are what cause these
people to attack their targets. The bully may be envious of
their target. Where envy is the reason behind bullying, it often
relates to qualifications, either professional or educational.
Through their constant criticism of others they seek to
deflect attention from their own deficiencies.

The threat may seem minor or trivial but to the bully with
unstable self-esteem, the attack may feel violent and the
reaction will be equally so. In their minds, these bullies are
reacting to protect themselves, rectify a wrong or punish a
slight. They may feel that their behaviour is justified and are
unlikely to accept that they initiated hostilities. Having
invented reasons to criticise others, they will invite others
to notice the target's 'incompetence' and will delight in
others joining in.

3 Socially incompetent bullies

This type of bully lacks the usual social skills we all need to
interact successfully with others. They may have poor

emotional control, self-awareness, and empathy, for example. These bullies may vent their anger regularly on their staff or colleagues by yelling at them or may gossip about or taunt their targets regularly.

They do this for several reasons:

- they cannot control themselves properly
- they are thoughtless about other people
- they don't appreciate what it is like on the receiving end

This type will exhibit surprise that they have been identified as a bully. They won't recognise many of the 'bullying events', as they have not intended any harm or even realised that their actions have upset people seriously.

4 'Micropolitical' bullies

These bullies are attempting to increase their influence and power through their bullying actions. They are rationally acting to improve their own position by undermining or attempting to eliminate others—often they feel they are acting strategically and competitively. They are likely to use behaviour that is encouraged by the organisation out of context.

Their main focus is their own success, however, rather than the detriment of their target. If the status quo changes, they may even attempt to forge coalitions with their previous targets, if they see this as the best strategy. They may use phrases such as 'it's business, not personal' or talk about the 'killer instinct' as a positive attribute.

5 'Pass the parcel' bullies

These bullies are under pressure that they just can't handle. They can be found in organisations that are downsizing. Robbed of job security, they lack the ability to say 'no' to their superiors when unreasonable demands are made. In order to achieve difficult targets they 'pass the parcel' and place ever-increasing workloads on their staff, passing on shorter deadlines that force them to work longer hours. The other parcel they are likely to pass is that of insecurity, making threats that they will fire those who don't toe the line.

For some, this is organisational bullying, since the bully is getting the same kind of treatment from his or her immediate boss. This group are often pitied rather than hated by their targets. They are between a rock and a hard place, but this does not excuse them from their duty of care to other employees. We all have choices about how to behave, and these bullies have chosen to pass the parcel.

This type of bullying can also come about where the organisational culture is one that encourages bullying. Through poor training and learning by poor example, managers and, to an extent, the workforce may even come to believe that bullying behaviour is the way to get things done.

Step three: Look at causes from inside your business

The concept of 'attribution theory' is an important one in the context of bullying. In essence, it states that if an experience is seen as positive, people will be keen to claim that they were in some way responsible for it. If the experience is seen as negative, people will be keen to suggest that others were responsible (Jones and Davies, 1965).

Bullying tends to have a polarising effect on our attributions. When a case comes to light, it's clear that witnesses include more references to the situation and attribute less to individuals than the targets do. In fact, the more persistent and severe the bullying, the stronger the target will attach blame to others. Where angry outbursts have taken place, anger is much more easily resolved and forgotten by bullies than targets, since the former had greater control over the event than the latter.

Escalation

Bullying experts often talk about the 'escalation' they see in various cases. This refers to the inability of the people involved to empathise with each other, calm the situation, and focus on shared goals. In fact, in the majority of cases the exact opposite happens: each party thinks that the situation is the fault of the other, continues to act as if their behaviour were entirely justified, and ignores any grounds for compromise. As a result, the target may be described as seeking revenge, while the bully may be seen to court trouble.

Step four: Look at the external causes

1 Tough environments

Where restructuring is happening, workload often increases for the remaining employees and the working environment becomes tougher. Where costs are being reduced and short contracts are replacing traditional employment, again, the context is harsher. In these environments you're at higher risk of being bullied because:

- fewer staff share increasing workloads
- efficiency drives ask staff to be more productive despite fewer resources
- increased targets lead to breaks being cut and staff working late

If the causes persist without action being taken to prevent them, bullying behaviour thrives.

2 Organisational bullying

Organisations that don't take action against bullying are encouraging their bullies. In surveys, the primary reason given for this behaviour happening at work is: 'The bullies do it because they can get away with it'.

If it is not directly sought out and tackled strongly, bullying will be used as a form of control and source of power. Oppressive and humiliating behaviour has a strongly negative effect on the health and morale of staff.

Theory X managers

Theory X was described by the management guru Douglas McGregor in 1960. It is used to describe the position adopted by some managers who believe that:

- employees are workshy
- employees crave security
- to get adequate effort from employees you need to direct, coerce, and control them, using punishments to get improvements

This set of beliefs makes authority central and where Theory X is the pervasive management style, bullying behaviour tends to be described as justified attempts to control employees. Where the distinction between bullying and control is not clarified, bullying culture tends to thrive.

Common mistakes

✗ **You're taken in by traditional stereotypes**

People may make the mistake of assuming that bullies are rather dull types with low self-confidence, who gain promotion through luck rather than merit. This is rarely the case. In reality, bullies tend not to lack self-confidence and are often highly skilled socially, often well liked by many. This adds to the difficulty of identifying them and preventing their appointment to posts in the organisation.

✗ **You think bullying is just down to personality**

Despite research into this area, there is little evidence to support individual personality as a predictor of bullying behaviour. Whilst factors such as aggression and self-esteem can play a part, it is often only in the interplay between two personalities in a particular situation that these become problematic. Also, other factors, such as empathy, may help reduce the effect of any possible 'clash'. Psychologists working in this area are always quick to warn that the complexity of personality makes it difficult to make useful predictions.

✗ **You think it's not bullying if you know the person well**

Sometimes people make the mistake of assuming that 'joshing' or joking within their workgroup is OK, even if it is persistently insulting and humiliating. Actually, bullying within the in-group has been found to be more disturbing and does greater harm to the targets than bullying by others. If you are a party to this type of bullying, do your best to make it stop.

STEPS TO SUCCESS

✓ Do realise that the role of intention is both important and complex. In some cases, bullying can turn out to have been unintentional.

✓ Understand that there are many types of bullies; they all behave in different ways and have different motives.

✓ Be aware of attribution theory: we attribute positive experiences to ourselves and negative experiences to others.

✓ Don't think you're being paranoid if you feel that the bullying you're experiencing is made up of many trivial events: this is the most common way that bullying begins.

✓ Understand that your work environment can play a big role in the prevalence of bullying: the tougher it is, the more bullying there's likely to be.

✓ Realise that in cultures where authority and control are central, bullying will thrive unless the distinction is clearly made between bullying and control.

Useful links

Association for Coaching:

www.associationforcoaching.com

British Association for Counselling and Psychotherapy:

www.bacp.co.uk

Understanding why bullies are picking on you

This chapter turns its attention away from the bullies themselves and on to their targets. People want to know what leads bullies to single them out for ill-treatment, but as we'll see below, there isn't one main issue: it can come from many reasons, but the most important thing to note is that no-one deserves to be bullied. Targets should not think that they themselves are causing the bullying, either consciously or unwittingly.

Step one: Understand why people are targeted

Sadly, no-one is bully-proof—bullies attack all types of people for different reasons, including:

- **gender.** Women and men are bullied in equal number in the United Kingdom, though the form that bullying takes is different. For example, more women than men report that bullying includes sexual harassment.
- **position.** As many people are bullied at the top of the organisational 'food chain' as they are at the bottom. The bullying may take very different forms, though the

effect is the same. Targets at the bottom of the hierarchy are more likely to be bullied by a group than those further up.

■ **ethnicity.** Ethnic minority groups have the highest incidence for all types of bullying behaviour. Targets from ethnic groups report exceptionally high incidences of insults and exclusion, compared to other targets.

■ **age.** Bullies most often pick on targets who are younger than them. Younger targets are less likely to stand up for themselves than more experienced members of staff, who often have the confidence and directness to challenge unacceptable behaviour when they encounter it. Naivety about the world of work will certainly make it hard for a target to recognise that they are being bullied or to find help when they do.

'Why me?': The unanswerable question

When you realise you're being bullied, it's entirely natural to ask yourself why you've become a target. Don't expect to find a cause by analysing yourself, though. It can be soul-destroying. Whether you're suffering yourself or trying to help someone else who is being bullied, focus instead on establishing the facts and show you are taking the matter seriously. If you're a manager, let the victim know that you can be trusted not to take sides and that you'll do something to resolve the situation.

Step two: Work out if you're a typical target

Bullying targets typically:

- are good at their jobs before the bullying starts, and are usually rated effective or high performing by their peers
- have good working relationships prior to bullying and are popular members of their teams
- are independent thinkers and workers, who are able to take the initiative
- have integrity, a well-defined set of standards to live by, and a strong sense of fair play
- have expertise in an area that is recognised by others and hold qualifications that the bully is envious of
- value feedback, paying more attention to external feedback than to their own gut feeling about how they are performing
- are hardworking and willing to go the extra mile
- are sensitive and empathic, concerned for others, and tolerant

Group bullying by peers is a little different. Where this happens, the targets are described as 'not fitting in'. This seems important at two levels:

- **'face doesn't fit'.** This affects people who are out of step regarding factors such as fashion, hobbies such as sporting interests, and personal hygiene. Diversity is not well tolerated by groups and bullying is a symptom of this.

■ **'not the way things are done around here'.** In this case, the target doesn't fit in with work-group norms. They may work harder than others or perhaps are brainier; they may be less motivated or need more help than others. Being different either has a negative effect on group performance or shows up relatively poor performance in the rest of the group. This makes the target intolerable to the bullies in the group who will try to push them out.

Step three: Understand what triggers bullying

The triggers for bullying episodes depend to some extent on the type of bully. They may be big events and moments of huge changes in the organisation or simply mark changes in the perception of the bully.

Examples of events are:

■ the arrival of a new boss
■ organisational restructuring
■ challenging goals being passed down to your boss
■ redundancies
■ the bully's previous target leaves

There are also some common 'red rags' to a bully, where he
or she feels that the target:

- is 'taking' his or her limelight
- has challenged him or her on a point of integrity
- is visibly having fun at work, winning the trust and
  respect of colleagues, staff, and clients
- is standing up for a colleague who is being bullied
- has been noticed for doing well or has gained a new
  qualification, award, or promotion
- has become a 'whistleblower' by reporting malpractice

Common mistakes

✗ You look at the target to get to the root of the bullying

It's a sad fact that some professions are much more
prone to bullying than others, and if you are targeted, it
could very simply be a matter of being in the wrong place
at the wrong time. Don't analyse the target to find out
why someone has been behaving badly towards them:
the bully is the problem, not the victim.

✗ You put bullying down to a clash of personalities

Some researchers have concluded that bullying is the
result of a personality clash. They report that targets are
more likely to be introverted, anxious, conscientious, and
submissive. These personality differences could be the

effect of bullying, however, rather than the original personality of the person. Certainly victims of bullying report that they *become* more withdrawn, anxious, obsessive about their work and less assertive, following the onset of bullying. Personality does not seem to be a useful factor to help us explain and prevent bullying.

STEPS TO SUCCESS

✓ Although targets are not perfect—no-one is—they themselves do not cause bullying.

✓ If you're a manager, remember that individuals from ethnic minority groups are most likely to report bullying, with especially high incidence of insults and exclusion.

✓ Look out for potential targets: they are usually competent in their field prior to bullying, but may not fit in with the rest of the group.

✓ In some cases, targets may not realise that they are being bullied.

✓ Don't dismiss bullying as nothing more than a personality clash—that would be to underestimate the seriousness of the problem.

✓ If you're a manager, don't dismiss reports of bullying without investigating properly first. Otherwise you'll actually increase the likelihood of more incidents of this type as the bully's confidence and power increases and the targets' faith in the system wanes.

Useful links

MIND National Association for Mental Health:
www.mind.org.uk
Success Unlimited:
www.successunlimited.co.uk

Rebuilding your confidence

This chapter will help targets of bullying to take stock of their situation and rebuild their confidence, before considering their options and deciding what course of action is best for them. Bullying has an undermining effect. Understanding what has happened to you is key to helping you back on your feet and the first step in the right direction.

Step one: Understand how bullying has its effect

Before we look at how you can start to rebuild your battered confidence, it's worth taking a step back and looking briefly at how bullying undermines most people's normal 'balance'.

As discussed in Chapters 1 and 2, the effects of bullying on a target can manifest themselves in many different ways. It can cause physical and mental stress as well as feelings of helplessness. For example, some targets find that while previously they were allowed plenty of latitude in the way they did their job, they are now being micro-managed by the bully and constantly scrutinised—this is likely to have a negative impact on their work.

TOP TIP

Having control over how to do your job and the freedom to take appropriate decisions is very empowering and helps to reduce stress at work. If this discretion is taken away, targets feel as if their protective support has been reduced and that they are out of kilter. As a result, they're more likely to be affected by stress.

Bullying becomes traumatic when it threatens our three fundamental assumptions about the world (Janoff-Bulman, 1992):

1 The world is benevolent and generally positive.

2 The world is meaningful and has logical rules, which are applied fairly.

3 The self is deserving of good treatment.

Bullying targets question their belief in the world being positive. They feel victimised by their bully and it may seem to them that witnesses are turning a blind eye or — worse still — joining in. Feelings of stress kick in as the targets experience uncertainty in their working relationships, and they also struggle with a hefty emotional workload as they try to adapt and keep their equilibrium while their perception of their work environment is changing.

If the bullying continues, the victims start to question the fairness of their employer or even the world in general. If they feel that their colleagues have failed to protect and support them, this feeling is compounded and targets are likely to experience strong emotions of confusion, anger, and sadness.

As time—and the bullying—goes on, targets may start to feel that others think badly of them, or that they deserve what they get from the bully. They start to think that they don't deserve any help or support, which in turn leads them to question their own worth. They may feel guilty about their anger towards others.

Some bullying victims report running over and over events in their mind, unable to resolve what is happening to them. This is an understandable reaction, but repeating that abuse and internalising it in this way can exacerbate the situation. In extreme cases, if the situation is not resolved, suicidal thoughts may occur, especially if a target feels that their job is central to his or her identity.

TOP TIP
**We are about to go on to how you can
start to get yourself out of this spiral of
confusion and negativity, but if you are a
victim of bullying and you have experienced
suicidal feelings, you must get help
immediately. No job is worth risking your
life for in this way, and no bully is worth this
level of upset. Remember that many bullies**

**are weak, selfish, and insecure people.
If anything, they are to be pitied, not feared.
Put yourself, your family, and your health first
and get some advice and support.**

Step two: Recognise the importance of taking action

It's time now to move our focus away from the negative experiences you've been through and on to ways you can begin to bring the balance back more in your favour.

There is a risk that your attempts to tackle the bullying you are suffering might not work, but taking action has been shown to have a positive effect on targets' health. It increases your perceived control over the situation, which can deflect some of the harmful effects of bullying.

Is 'doing nothing' ever an option?

If you're subjected to a single episode of bullying, letting the matter drop may be a valuable option. Reacting against an unusual event may cause more harm than good, by escalating events.

However, 'doing nothing' is an unwise choice if bullying persists. Take action early while you are able, as research shows that it is the most effective way to stop bullying. It goes without saying that you'll need to gather up all your courage to do this, but it's much easier to tackle a problem at the outset than it is once it has become an established pattern. For the sake of your physical health, psychological well-being, your job, and your relationships at home and at work, make a stand. Don't be afraid to get help if you need it, as step three shows.

Step three: Seek some help

When you're ready to tackle the bullying, confide in someone. Choose someone whom you trust, who knows you well, and who can give you a reality check. Support may also come from unexpected angles — someone who you may not be that close to, but who may have noticed what's happening to you or who may have been through something similar him- or herself.

Here are some ideas about where to seek help and how it may help you:

■ specialist websites dealing with workplace bullying can be a helpful first port of call and can give you up-to-date information about your rights and sources of further help

■ a counsellor, therapist, or coach who specialises in work stress can give you practical help in finding a solution to your situation. They can also help you to distinguish

between the objective facts of the case and your
emotional reaction to them

■ a specialist legal expert can offer a view as to whether
you can win a case

■ close friends or loved ones can be there for you and give
you emotional support

■ colleagues (where possible) can give you back-up, or
can act as witnesses. However, they may be intimidated
by your bully and also have to act to protect their own
interests. Don't take it personally if they won't get
involved: this may reinforce the belief that you are all
working in a climate of fear

■ occupational health or union representatives may have
direct experience in helping other employees and need
to know about bullying in the organisation to help protect
others

■ your GP may help you obtain a proper break, as well as
offering symptomatic relief from the effects you are
suffering

Step four: Protect yourself

Given the effect that bullying can have on your health, it is
very important not to escalate the situation through your
actions. Whether you are a witness, a target, or are trying to

give the target support to resolve the situation, **protect yourself**. A bully is likely to turn on anyone they see as a threat. Be careful whom you confide in. Also be aware that many bullies are well connected, and steer clear of your bully's allies.

Don't change your work patterns, as longer hours will not help the situation. The better your performance, the more work you do, the more you threaten your bully. Also, the more tired you are, the less prepared you are to protect yourself from further abuse.

TOP TIP

However low you feel, don't retaliate or seek revenge as you'll undermine your credibility. Instead, remain professional. Keep a note of the bullying behaviour and its effect upon you so that you can back up your story to your manager if you need to. Don't get obsessed with noting the tiniest details or running over and over the bullying in your mind: just make a quick note and try to move on.

Keeping strong

Obviously, your stress levels will rocket if you are going through a difficult time. Don't ignore this, but combat the stress through any methods you know work for you. By taking action, you'll feel that you're increasing your control over one part of the situation at least.

For example:

- boost your self-esteem by reminding yourself of all your past achievements in less toxic environments
- build roles away from the workplace that give you an alternative source of self-respect and identity
- keep physically fit. Exercise gives a degree of protection against the harmful effects of bullying.

Step five: Work out the severity of the bullying

When you're in the thick of things it can be hard to take stock and see objectively what is happening to you.
To help you identify the severity of your situation, ask yourself:

- Is the bullying a barrier to my performance at work?
- Will the bully prevent me getting a promotion or being given other career opportunities within the organisation?
- Is the bullying interfering with the way I think about myself?
- Does the bullying affect my home life and well-being?

If the question is 'yes' to these questions, you need urgent help to resolve the situation. Consider the two questions below, which may help to put things in perspective:

- What will it cost you to carry on coping with your bully's behaviour?
- What will it cost you to leave?

Step six: Acknowledge your feelings

Take a moment to think about how you feel, as decision-making is an emotional as well as a rational process. What are the main issues and how do you feel about these? Write down words that describe your reactions to the important issues facing you. When you have finished, review what you have written and try to understand what has prompted these emotions. Write this down too.

This is important work for two reasons:

- if you decide to stay in your current job, you need to come to terms with your reactions and find strategies for coping better in the future
- if you decide to move on, you will need to deal with and park these issues and emotions for good

Step seven: Believe in yourself

Humans are born with very few fears: babies feel fear when they hear loud noises and are startled by sudden movements because they fear falling. Very soon they learn to fear hunger and to fear being alone. We build new fears on things that have caused us pain or discomfort.

Fear is a learned response to our past environment. But sometimes the fear is unhelpful and constrains us in the present from what we want or need to do. When fear becomes a barrier, we need to learn to overcome it and the foundation for that learning is self-belief.

Know that you have the power to learn a different response. By facing what you fear and acting with your mind in the present, you allow different responses and reactions to those of the past. Each time you face your fear you free yourself from your past. That does not mean that you should continue to endure bullying, but that you need to face what is happening to you and then take action to ensure your future is different.

Common mistakes

✗ You attack your bully

Keep your cool and don't allow things to escalate through your actions. Write down what has happened from the start, focusing on what the bully's negative behaviours were and the effect they had on you. Get help to do this if you need to.

It's very easy for people who are not currently being bullied to imagine themselves being very proactive against a bully. When they actually are in a bullying situation, though, they're unable to carry out these actions as fear sets in.

To see things in their true light and find the right route forwards, you'll need support and space. Take some time off if you can and spend some time reflecting on the feedback you received before you met your bully. Bullies tend to pick on high flyers, people who have high standards. Don't question your ability, but focus on what you can do to get a healthy working environment again.

STEP TO SUCCESS

✔ Don't blame yourself: the targets of bullying are never responsible for the victimisation. That doesn't mean they are saints, naturally, just that it is the bully who is at fault, not the victim.

✔ Taking action to resolve the situation has a protective effect: it will help to re-establish the control that victims feel has been taken away from them.

✔ 'Doing nothing' can be an option if you feel that the incident was a genuine one-off, but if it becomes clear that the bullying is ramping up, take action quickly.

✔ If you are being bullied, acknowledge your feelings about the situation and try to work through why you react the way you do.

✔ Get some help. Talk to your manager, friends, family, trusted colleagues, the HR department, or a specialist helpline if you need to. You don't have to face this issue on your own.

✔ Remain professional at all times, even if it's the last thing you feel like doing. Retaliating to the bully often adds grist to his or her mill. That doesn't mean that you should ignore what is happening, but don't give the bully anything else to hit back at you about. Make a note of what has happened and when and use it to back up a complaint if you choose to make one (see Chapter 5).

✔ Try to set aside past fears and future concerns. Focus on the present moment and what you can do now to change things positively.

Useful links

Bully Online:
www.bullyonline.org
Bullying Institute:
www.bullyinginstitute.org

Thinking about moving on

Moving on is the first of the two main options that victims of bullying can use to get back into a healthy working environment. In this chapter, we'll look at why people might choose this route and how they can make their transition a really positive step.

Step one: Understand why targets move on

There are many reasons why someone who has been bullied might decide to move on to pastures new.

For example, some targets decide to look for a new job because their health has been impaired and they have been signed off work for a long recuperation. Once recovered, they may not want to return to their previous position, especially if the bully is still there. In some cases, a leaving settlement with the organisation allows them to start afresh.

Some sufferers of bullying leave their job because they realise that the bullying is damaging their confidence and their career. They move to avoid their bully. Others feel that their bully is trying to get them sacked. They may decide that it is better to take a risk and jump ship before they are pushed out.

Some victims see that their career is blocked as long as they have a bully for a manager and seek work elsewhere to get on with the rest of their lives. If you are thinking of leaving your bully behind, you're not alone: 25% of targets leave as a result of bullying, and 20% of those who have *witnessed* bullying also leave because of it.

Reaction of targets

Targets' patterns of reaction are not simple in the face of bullying. Research has found that, typically, they will try a series of coping strategies, including:

- showing their loyalty to the workgroup by redoubling efforts
- voicing their grievance
- neglecting their work
- reducing their interest and involvement in their workgroup
- finally, leaving their job

These strategies aren't necessarily used in this order but in a complex way, as the employee tries different tactics to get a constructive result. Certainly an organisation that is actively on the lookout for bullies has plenty of opportunities to notice what is happening and do something to help.

Step two: Think through your concerns about leaving

There's no doubt about it, it is a difficult decision to make. Some targets feel guilty about moving on and worry about leaving behind colleagues who are also being bullied or leaving clients in the lurch. Sometimes these concerns keep people in their job longer than they may have planned.

If you feel this way, your loyalty is misplaced and undervalued. Your first concern must be for yourself and your own health and well-being.

Think of it this way:

■ leaving can help other targets, by reminding them that it is an option
■ leaving can help the organisation by letting them know that they have a problem, particularly if you ask for an exit interview and tell your boss or human resources department why you're leaving
■ taking control protects your mental and physical well-being
■ putting your health and well-being before your financial security is a positive step—how can you earn your living if you become seriously ill?
■ moving on is not an overreaction but a sensible decision to unblock your career

■ if you are being bullied, the grass really is greener elsewhere

Recognising the right time to leave a job is difficult. The trick is to be clear about what is important to you. Once your priorities and goals are established, the decision becomes much clearer.

Step three: Know what you want

If you've been through a traumatic time at the hands of workplace bullies, avoiding bullying in your next role is likely to be a priority. Expressed positively, you are looking for a constructive work environment, where employees feel valued. Some sectors and occupations are better than others. An international review of a number of studies summarised the findings on bullying in the workplace as follows:

' . . . a higher risk of being bullied is reported for the social and health, public administration and education sectors, which all belong to the public sector.'

(Zapf, Einarsen, Hoel and Vartia, 2003)

In the United Kingdom, there are other clusters of high-risk jobs, for example in dance or the hotel industry. If you are in a high-risk occupation, you may want to consider a career change. Think back to when you took your job:

- What factors attracted you to it?
- What did you like about the work?
- What did you like about the sector?

Do these factors still sound attractive? If they don't, why not think about a career change? Many people change careers successfully—sometimes quite radically—even late in their working life.

You may decide that you love your work and want to continue in the successful career path that you had before the bullying started. Don't be put off because it is a high-risk occupation. Just do your research well before taking your next role and seek out employers who have an anti-bullying policy.

As a useful exercise, divide a sheet of paper in four. Use it to note the factors that you are looking for in your next job. For example:

1 What kind of organisation do you want to work for? Think about what you would like in terms of size, sector, environment, philosophy, attitude to staff, prospects for learning, and opportunities for promotion.

2 What are the ingredients of the ideal role? What would its main focus be? What strengths would you like to use? Would you like to work full or part-time?

3 What do you want in a boss? Hands on or hands off? A

mentor? Someone with a consultative style or who
gives a prescriptive lead?

4 What will make up your ideal package? Consider basic
pay, bonus, car, holidays, relocation, flexible working
options, and overtime.

Now you have a checklist against which you can do a 'reality
check'.

Step four: Choose the right time

You may have decided to leave your job but it may not be the
right moment to hand in your notice. Choosing the right one
will depend on your situation, including:

- how serious the bullying is
- how badly you are suffering
- the state of the job market
- the state of your finances

In terms of your bank balance, it's often best to look for a
new job before you leave your present one. Your CV will have
no gaps between employment dates this way, which you
might feel is best.

On the other hand, if you've suffered from extreme bullying,
you might benefit more from taking a leap of faith, handing
in your notice, and having some time to recover before
you start job-hunting in earnest. Turn your anger into

action and your pain into resolution to get the great job you
deserve.

TOP TIP

**Make sure you allow yourself the time to get
rid of the negative feelings associated with
your previous job. If it means that you can talk
at interview about your last job without tears,
discomfort, or visible anger, taking time out
will prove a sound decision.**

If taking time out just isn't possible because of your financial
situation but you can't face being at work, it may be possible
for you to take sick leave if your health is suffering. Your GP
may also be able to arrange counselling, which can help you
to cope better with your current situation and move on
emotionally. These factors will also make job-hunting easier
and more successful.

Whatever you decide to do, don't suffer in silence. There is
help out there and no shame in asking for it. No-one should
have to endure bullying. Don't allow the situation to worsen;
seek help now and leave your bully in your past.

Step five: Investigate what's out there

It's time to review the market. Start with a list of the options
and ask yourself for each one: what do I need to know about
this to decide if it is for me? Then decide how you will get that

information: via the Internet, a contact, a professional body or another way? When this list is finished use it as an action list. As you research the options, some will start to look more and more interesting, while you may find barriers or sticking points for other options. As you research, the list usually gets shorter, although you may discover more options as you go.

Next, find out how available these options are in your area. Scan your newspapers, call two or three recruitment agencies, and visit the websites of some relevant companies. You may decide to change job when the market is at its most competitive or you may decide to hang on in there at your present job until the market picks up and the chances of your getting the role you want increase.

The more people you talk to about opportunities, the 'luckier' you'll become. This is especially the case if you are prepared to discuss your skills and strengths and have an up-to-date CV to hand. Job seekers often undervalue their network of contacts or fail to recognise that they have a network, yet for experienced people it is the most fruitful route to the next job.

Common mistakes

✗ **You jump out of the frying pan and into the fire**

Accepting the first role that is offered to get away from an unbearable situation may seem fine at first. If the decision has been rushed, however, it can turn out to be a nightmare. Go carefully through a reality check. Do some research before you move to another organisation. Ask to talk to some members of the department you will be joining. Better still, ask to talk to the person who held the job before you to satisfy yourself that it is the right decision for you, before you sign on the dotted line.

✗ You don't have the confidence to negotiate

If you are too keen to get a new job, you may feel that you should just take what is offered, no questions asked. Remember the skills, knowledge, and experience that you are bringing to your new role. If you have a job offer, treat it as proof that the employer wants or needs these strengths and don't forget to ask yourself:

- Will I be happy with this package in 6 months' time?
- Is this pay above or below the average for the market?
- Is this pay similar or different to that of my future colleagues?
- Given my skills and experience, is this the right level of pay?
- Will I still be happy if I am asked to work a lot of overtime?

Wait until you get the written contract. Perhaps there are elements that you have identified in your reality check as not quite right for you. Make a list of them and call your potential future employer to ask what can be done to improve these elements. Be very clear that you are interested in the role, so the employer does not feel they are being given an ultimatum.

Remind them of what you will be bringing, in terms of your strengths and the ways in which the role fits your profile. Allow them time to come back to you with a better offer. Be flexible and know which points you're willing to compromise on, but don't be pushed on the core points.

STEPS TO SUCCESS

✓ Moving on may be the easiest way to get on with the rest of your life after bullying.

✓ If you do decide to move, make sure you leave behind all the negative emotions associated with the bullying episodes. Be positive and look forward to starting again with a clean slate elsewhere.

✓ You may feel guilty about leaving colleagues and clients behind if you choose to leave your job, but put yourself, your family, and your health first.

✓ Make yourself a checklist describing what you want from your next role. This will be a useful tool when it comes to measuring new offers that come your way.

✓ People *do* change careers: it's not at all unusual these days, and you can change career too if you feel that's what's right for you.

✔ As well as using all the traditional job-hunting channels, use your network of contacts—usually people are glad to help if they can.

Useful links

Anywork Anywhere:
www.anyworkanywhere.com
Daily Telegraph careers section:
www.jobs.telegraph.co.uk
Fish4jobs:
www.fish4jobs.co.uk
Gojob:
www.gojobsite.com
Hays:
www.hays-ap.com
Jobsite:
www.jobsite.co.uk
Manpower:
www.manpower.co.uk
Monster:
www.monster.co.uk
Reed:
www.reed.co.uk
Total Jobs:
www.totaljobs.com
Workthing:
www.workthing.com

Making a stand

If moving isn't the right option for you, making a stand where you are is the other route you could investigate. This often means pursuing a formal grievance internally or taking legal action against your employer. Do be prepared for a long and tough fight, though.

Step one: Know that your organisation has responsibilities

Under UK law, employers have a duty to provide a safe workplace for their employees. Bullying at work is recognised as a cause of stress by the Health and Safety Executive. The Health and Safety at Work Act 1974 can be used to hold employers liable for subjecting employees to work conditions that foreseeably cause psychological injury.

Laws relating to unfair dismissal and constructive dismissal have also been used successfully to seek redress against employers who have subjected an employee to severe mistreatment. The employer, in this type of case, must be deemed to have breached the implied terms of the contract by allowing bullying to continue after a grievance has been raised.

In most cases, it will help your case if you have reported the bullying and its effect on you. Your employer may respond quickly and effectively to resolve the situation when informed about bullying problems you are facing. By law, bullying should be tackled by employers and dealt with in the same way as any other safety hazard at work.

However, the most common experience of targets who report bullying is that nothing happens. In fact, more often the bullying gets worse rather than better. There is evidence to suggest that reporting bullying to trade union representatives or to personnel staff is most likely to improve the situation, and so this would therefore seem the safest option.

TOP TIP

If you decide to stay and fight your bully, you have a responsibility to protect yourself and others: tell someone about the bullying situation, preferably trade union representatives or personnel staff, who are trained to deal with it professionally. Representatives of Employee Safety (ROES) or occupational health workers should also be able to help you if you consult them.

Step two: Know what you want

As with most situations, knowing what you want to achieve is the best starting point you can have. In bullying cases, targets typically want something along the lines of:

- **normality.** 'I want things to be how they were before I encountered my bully.'
- **apology.** 'I want my bully to recognise and apologise for their actions.'
- **public apology.** 'I want my bully to be humiliated by their actions.'
- **financial redress.** 'I want to be given a sum of money to compensate me for the pain and humiliation I have endured because of my bully.'
- **vengeance.** 'I want to see my bully laid low and I'll enjoy watching their pain.'

If you find yourself fantasising about vengeance, hold it right there. Has your bully altered your thinking to the extent where you dream of being a bully yourself? Be careful what you wish for.

At the other end of the scale, normality is unlikely to be possible within the same department. It is more usual for the target to be moved into another role than it is for the bully to be moved.

Is confrontation an option?

Confrontation is a good option where bullying is recent and not a well-established pattern of behaviour.

This is the most successful way to make bullying stop, but it has to be done *before* the pattern of bullying has become established.

Make sure you are prepared. Be clear about what you are going to say and how you will say it. A quiet, reasonable, business-like tone is likely to be most effective, unless you work in a very noisy environment.

1 State the bullying behaviour and the effect of that behaviour on you.
2 State that it is not acceptable to you.
3 Suggest that you are not an easy target.
4 Using a non-threatening manner, remind your bully of the law.

For example:
1 'Recently you have started to ignore and belittle my contributions in team meetings, which I find hurtful and upsetting. You have also started to make unpleasant comments about me to others, which has made me angry.'
2 'I don't think it is an acceptable or professional way to behave. I consider it to be bullying.'
3 'If you have a problem, we can discuss it like adults. I am not going to be bullied, so you won't find me an easy target.'
4 'In law, employees have a duty of care to one another. If you continue to mistreat me I'll make a formal complaint, but I would rather we sort this out now between ourselves.'

It is best used soon after the onset of bullying. Why? Because where bullying has become a habit, it can lead to an increase in negative behaviours, with damaging effects upon the victim. Many targets don't recognise what is happening early enough to use this route, but research has shown that those who have been successful at stopping bullying confronted their bullies very quickly to voice their non-acceptance.

Step four: Change your reactions

If what you are currently doing isn't stopping your bully from mistreating you, change the way you react to him or her. Keep your cool and stay professional. There is no suggestion that you appease your bully by changing your working pattern—quite the opposite. Do what you can do within normal limits and then go home and put your bully out of your mind.

Go back to the section on the different types of bully and their motives. What reaction is your bully getting from you that makes it pleasurable? Can you respond in a different way, to make bullying you less interesting?

Step five: Collect evidence

If you intend to start formal grievance procedures against your bully, or if you are considering taking your employer to tribunal or court, you'll need evidence. Keep a diary of incidents, focusing on the behaviour and its effect upon you. An example is given on pp. 60–61. You don't need every last detail, just enough to establish the pattern, even if the individual events may look trivial.

Date and time	Situation and witnesses	Behaviour	Effect on me
1st May, 8.30	Handed Boss my design Daphne	Barely acknowledged it, let alone thanked me for saving his bacon	Fear that he might shout at me again, as he did on Friday. Relief that he didn't. Cross that all my effort this weekend was ignored.
1st May, 9.30	Meeting with clients Boss chairing meeting John and Sonia	Ignored my attempts to contribute important information. Interrupted me twice. Passed off my idea for the design as his own.	Frustrated, angry. Had to catch up with two senior team members after the meeting to give them the information.

Date and time	Situation and witnesses	Behaviour	Effect on me
1st May, 12.00	Lunch with clients John	Several belittling comments to clients centring around me being 'the newest team member and therefore she doesn't yet know anything of value' with phoney paternal look on his face.	Furious, embarrassed, constantly undermined. Couldn't do anything about it in front of clients.
1st May, 15.15	Meeting with clients Daphne	Dismissed to write up the report by tomorrow with full details! Couldn't argue because of the clients being there.	Shattered, emotional. Stayed up till 1am to finish report.

TOP TIP

Do take care that you don't get obsessed with diarising the bullying episodes—it can add further stress by forcing you to chew over unpleasant events. If you find it useful to get thoughts out of your head and onto paper, the diary can be useful, but try to keep a lid on things. Make your notes for as long as you feel appropriate, but don't re-read them constantly.

If you are intending to use your report internally to persuade the management to take action, it may also be useful to collect evidence that:

- bullying is affecting others' performance too
- morale is low
- high staff turnover is due to culture of fear
- recruitment and training costs could be cut by improving culture

Collect witness statements and ask your colleagues for support. Try to be understanding if they are fearful, looking after their own interests, or if they just can't see the problem. There is a chance that you may alienate some colleagues but reiterate that the statements are key to stopping the bullying and are essential in court.

If they won't give you a statement, write a short description of the situation yourself. Send them a copy.

Ask them to correct it or let you know in writing if they disagree with it.

TOP TIP
If you feel able, ask your bully for clarification after an incident. Get down in writing the tasks and deadlines that have been set or ask for more specific feedback in writing.
Together with your diary of incidents, this 'paper trail' will give proof that the bullying took place.

Step six: Prepare a complaint

If your company holds a personnel file on you, ask to see it before you make your complaint. Make notes or get copies of both positive and negative documents.

Does your organisation have an anti-bullying policy and a formal grievance procedure related to it? Do you have clear evidence and witnesses who are willing to make statements and support you? A formal complaint is only recommended if it seems that the route will be fruitful; if the bullying cannot be proven, a warning may be given, but there's no guarantee. It's also likely that the complaint will escalate the bullying if the bully thinks he or she can get away with it. The target can end up worse off than before, being less able to prove that the bullying is continuing.

Formal notification starts the grievance procedure. In large organisations the employee handbook can help. By linking your complaint to company policy, you can make your grievance more persuasive. Focus on objective statements and give examples. Lay out bullying behaviour that you are experiencing and its effects. State where company policy is contravened and add a strong statement about your strengths and achievements and results.

If grievance procedure states your manager is first port of call and your manager is the bully, go to his or her manager instead. If you're in doubt, go to colleagues in Human Resources, to senior management, or even to the board. These people have a duty of care to you as their employee.

The legal route

If the grievance procedure yields no help and nothing changes, you could take your organisation to court. But be realistic. Find out what is involved and the likely outcomes before starting a formal action. Cases rarely come to court and compensation is also rare.

There are three big questions that you need to answer:

1 What will it cost you (in financial terms and in terms of your health)?
2 Are you likely to succeed (in terms of getting an outcome that will help you)?
3 Is the outcome worth the risk?

Targets who take their cases to court report that the procedure is very tough. It is likely that you would suffer increased stress from this route. Having said that, some people may feel better for taking action and the possibility of a financial settlement (though uncommon) can help.

Step seven: Consider your options

Why do targets stay? There are practical reasons: most people are reliant on the pay and benefits they receive. Targets may believe that the situation will get better soon. They may look back on happier times with the organisation and expect that things will blow over if they keep their nose to the grindstone. They may need to find a new job before they can leave, which can be hard to do while suffering bullying. Taking time off to attend interviews with other companies may not seem a very good idea; if the bully is their manager, for example, it could give him or her ammunition. If targets are close to retirement age, changing jobs may have an adverse effect on their pension.

Reputation also plays a large role in this decision. If someone is proud of his or her reputation at work, he or she may not take much more sick leave than other employees, even when suffering badly. Targets may be worried about references or how it would look on their CV if they take extended sick leave or walk out of their job. It may even become a matter of pride, to prove that they can cope with anything. It may be a way of clinging on to some self-esteem: 'despite everything, I stuck it out, I didn't walk away.'

TOP TIP
Some bullying victims may also decide to stay on because they no longer have the self-confidence for job hunting; their self-belief may have been brought so low that they don't feel able to get another job. The psychological effects of bullying may also have left them very angry, wanting revenge, and unable to leave before they have it.

Step eight: Realise that formal procedures aren't always best

Should you use formal methods of redress? In some situations you cannot win and the process is extremely stressful. Some targets will be determined to see their bully brought to justice but although company policies and the law are changing, the way things stand at the moment, the outcome is rarely worth the strain.

When you are feeling bruised or depressed, it can be hard to come up with a logical argument for anything, never mind the potential strain of a pursuing someone through the courts or through a formal disciplinary hearing. It will make you feel better, and more in control, if you try to impose some order on the turmoil you have been through. As you analyse the best solution for you, ask yourself:

- What will the winning outcome be?
- What is the benefit of this outcome?
- Can I win?
- Can I cope with the process?
- What will the cost be?
- What are the other options?
- What are the benefits of the other options?
- What is the cost of other options?
- What looks like the best route for me?

TOP TIP
Think through your exit strategy and make sure you have a fall-back position. Even if your intention is to stay and fight, you may find that as an internal or legal process moves forward, your position becomes untenable. Think through your strategy and be prepared to use your back-up plan if things don't turn out as you'd expected.

Common mistakes

✗ You turn your anger on to yourself

Targets who stay in their role are at risk from themselves as well as their bully. Constantly running through bullying episodes, fantasising different outcomes or plotting your bully's downfall can induce as much stress as the original. Of course you have a right to be angry but don't let yourself become obsessed by your bully. Protect yourself from self-bullying through repetition.

Instead, use your angry energy in the gym or swimming pool—or take up kickboxing! Exercise is a great way to fight stress. But whatever you do, try to always keep your cool in front of your bully. Get help and support while you sort things out.

STEPS TO SUCCESS

✔ Remember that UK law obliges employers to provide a safe working environment.

✔ If you are being bullied, your employer has a health and safety problem that they need to know about: if you can't tell them yourself, get help to do it.

✔ Work out what you want to happen: what does a good solution look like to you?

✔ Confront your bully early on if you can. Once a pattern of bullying has been established, confrontation can escalate the bullying.

✔ See if you can spot what reaction your bully is enjoying and then change your reactions to make bullying you less interesting.

✔ Collect evidence: diary entries and witness statements are especially useful if you can get them.

✔ If you decide to make a formal complaint through work channels, link it with your company's anti-bullying policy and focus your letter on specific behaviours and their effects on you.

✔ Make sure your CV is up to date and that your financial matters are sorted out, in case you need to leave your job at short notice.

Useful links

Just Fight On:
www.jfo.org.uk
Trades Union Congress (TUC):
www.tuc.org.uk

Whistleblowing

Whistleblowing is bringing to attention a dangerous or illegal practice that the whistleblower discovers through his or her work. One of the most famous whistleblowers of recent times is Jeffrey Wigand, who exposed malpractice in the tobacco industry and was portrayed by Russell Crowe in the 1999 film *The Insider*.

Whistleblowing can be viewed as a valuable activity: it can improve the way organisations work and protect the public from unsafe, unfair, or illegal work methods. However, some organisations and employees may view whistleblowing as disloyal and harmful, especially when it damages their reputation or is not in their immediate interest. In the United Kingdom, the Public Interest Disclosure Act 1998 (PIDA) is used to make sure that messengers are not shot, but that their messages are acted upon.

Step one: Understand UK law on whistleblowing

In summary, PIDA protects most workers from dismissal and victimisation following their whistleblowing actions.

It encourages people to channel their concern about unsafe or illegal activities (or cover-ups of these) to the correct people within the organisation. If no action is taken and the activities continue—or if the whistleblower is too fearful of the consequences if they raise the alarm internally—a list of prescribed regulators are the next port of call and PIDA protects these disclosures. If the matter is still not cleared up satisfactorily, then wider public disclosures, such as statements made to the police or newspapers, will be protected.

Although not designed to prevent or stop bullying, the importance of PIDA is that:

- it facilitates the exposure of unsafe practices, including bullying, that are a danger to the health and safety of employees
- it protects whistleblowers from being victimised or sacked as a result of making disclosures about malpractice, provided that they are not made for personal gain
- where a whistleblower is victimised or dismissed, compensation for losses suffered are uncapped and an element for aggravated damages may also be awarded by an employment tribunal
- gagging clauses are deemed void where they conflict with the Act

Step two: Understand what PIDA means for your organisation

Under the terms of PIDA, employers will no longer be in a position to plead ignorance of malpractice since the effect of the Act is to ensure that disclosures are made and logged. Organisations will be held accountable on the basis of actual rather than implied knowledge.

Employers will need to develop a whistleblowing policy and procedure, so that witnesses to bullying (or any other danger or malpractice) have encouragement to come forward to managers within the organisation before damage is done. Having the protection of the law and being able to raise the issue of bullying internally in this way means that complainants can act without fear of being victimised or sacked.

Step three: Get ready to blow the whistle

Public Concern at Work (PCaW), the independent whistleblowing charity (and now a registered legal advice centre), states that protection is virtually automatic under PIDA where a worker, having concerns about malpractice, *raises the matter internally first* or with the person responsible for the malpractice.

If you feel that whistleblowing is an appropriate course of action for you to take, contact PCaW for individual advice. PCaW's general UK telephone advice line can be reached at 020 7404 6609; if you are based in Scotland, you can also call 0141 883 6761. They will:

■ help you to think through the risks and possible outcomes of different options
■ ask you about the facts of the case and advise you how to raise a concern effectively

Who should I speak to?

Depending on the size of the business you work for, you could:

■ go to union representatives or a staff association
■ go to management (if the bully is your boss, go to his or her manager)
■ go to personnel staff
■ go to the board

Remember that the goal is to get the organisation to take action to stop the bullying, which is a risk to the safety of the work environment. Don't give up but don't put yourself in a risky position either, as that would help no-one.

If internal routes fail, a riskier route is to go to the Prescribed Regulator—in bullying cases this is the Health and Safety Executive.

You could also turn to the police. They would record a dispute and, depending on the circumstances, talk to all parties first to understand the matter. An official cautionary letter may be sent or if matters are more serious, they may charge someone with assault, harassment, or criminal damage charges. They will need evidence, which is often difficult to provide in bullying cases, but will not be dismissive in cases where it is hard to prove that bullying has taken place.

It is still more risky to take up the matter externally, however: an employer may suggest that by doing so, you have made your position untenable and it is certainly not seen as a good career move by other managers. As far as bullies are concerned, by contacting the police you have attacked them and their reputation. This is likely to escalate the bullying while at the same time driving it underground, thus making it harder to prove that it is continuing. This may put you in a more dangerous position than you were in before. If you have been unable to prove the bullying in the eyes of the law, you may be branded as a troublemaker, which could hurt you still further.

Common mistakes

✗ **You forget that targets may not be grateful for their rescue**

The moment when a target labels him or herself as 'bullied' may be either very difficult or therapeutic. It may take the bullying victim some time to come to terms with thinking of themselves in this way and in fact some psychologists suggest that it may be best not to use the term 'bullied' if the targets are not using it themselves. Others suggest that it may be a positive first step towards realising that the problem is not a personal one, and it may even hasten a resolution of the situation. Either way, be warned that the target may feel further picked on by the label of 'victim'—Try to be as understanding as you can if this is the case for you.

STEPS TO SUCCESS

✔ Whistleblowing is raising concerns about crimes or malpractice in the workplace.

✔ It gives valuable information about what is happening within the organisation to the people who have the power to change things.

Useful links

Health and Safety Executive:

www.hse.gov.uk

Public Concern at Work:

www.pcaw.co.uk

Breaking the chain

Bullying practices have no place in the modern workplace. When you consider that many thousands of targets are severely distressed and become seriously ill every year through bullying, it focuses the mind. If you are not a manager, you may be wondering what use this chapter will be for you. But each and every employee in an organisation can play an important role in wiping out bullying.

Organisations' typical reactions to reports of bullying are at best unhelpful and frequently worsen the situation for the victims. According to Gary Namie, an expert on workplace bullying, 32% of organisations, on learning that they have a bullying problem, worsen it by reacting negatively to the target, while 51% do nothing.

Doing nothing is not an option as it strengthens the bullies' power. Enlightened organisations are leading the way in their efforts to keep bullying in the past. Their work on best practice policies and procedures is certainly having an effect. Here we discuss what can be done from different angles to break the chain.

Step one: Take action as a colleague

What can you do when someone reports bullying to you?

✔ Listen very carefully and ask questions to find out exactly what has been happening and for how long. It may help later if you make a few notes.

✔ Ask the target what help they need and help them to find it.

✔ Even if the target's assessment of the situation is not flawless, support his or her main argument that the bullying behaviour is not acceptable. Help them look at their options.

Frequently the target will feel trapped and unable to act or get help. Going through the options will help them to regain a feeling of control, which can protect them from the worst effects of bullying. Examples of choices they can make are:

■ staying or leaving
■ fighting or lying low
■ acting independently or seeking the help of others
■ using formal support channels (a trade union, for example) or informal ones (friends); lodging a formal grievance or having a quiet chat with occupational health workers or a personnel manager

✔ Protect yourself, but do what you can to help.

✔ If the bullying has just started, you can help a victim to confront their bully. Revisit Chapter 6 for more help on this.

✔ Fulfil your duty of care to others in the workplace by bringing the situation to the attention of others. See Chapter 7.

✔ If the target suggests retaliation, advise them that this might antagonise the bully and make the situation worse.

✔ Suggest that the safest way to get help may be through your company's personnel department, or a union representative.

✔ Drawing attention to the problem is important for the safety of other employees as well as the person under immediate threat.

✔ No-one is perfect, but reassure the target of their worth.

✔ Get specific case-by-case advice on how to help the target from UK National Workplace Bullying Advice Line (01235 212286) or Public Concern at Work, the whistleblowing charity (020 7404 6609).

Step two: Take responsibility

If you have been accused of bullying or know that your work methods have left people trampled in your wake, this section is for you. Previous sections have looked at how external factors, such as a tough environment, can increase (but not excuse) bullying. Internal factors are also important, such as empathy and self-awareness but a bully cannot respond to an accusation with 'I don't have very good people skills.' It just isn't good enough.

Bullies *are* sometimes unaware how people see their negative behaviour towards others. They may not even be aware that their behaviour *is* negative. It is what they do when they receive the feedback that defines them. Many individuals, having discovered that they are seen as bullies, have learned how to manage their behaviour. They have gone on to become an asset to their organisation, rather than a liability.

When did you last think about your working style and how you come across? Do *you* need to change? Be completely honest and ask yourself:

- Do you make or join in with jokes at others' expense?
- Do you visibly display your anger and frustration?
- Are you rude or very blunt in your criticism or give strong negative feedback in front of others?
- Do you pass on rumours about others?

- Have you made strategic moves to interfere with another's work?
- Are you 'passing the parcel', delegating more than workers can handle?
- Have you increased other pressures on your team?
- Have you increased demand, whilst ignoring constraints?
- If your staff want to discuss things, do you tell them to 'just get on with it'?
- Do you enjoy a heated argument?
- Have you been taking out your own stress on others?
- Are you using a very authoritarian style?
- Do you like to have control of everything, including how work is performed?
- Have you withheld information deliberately to make others look bad?

If you answered:

- 'yes' or 'yes, regularly', you could be a bully. You need to change how you behave.
- 'sometimes', you're on shaky ground. Seek feedback and act on it.
- 'rarely' or 'not at all', you're in the safest territory

As discussed in Chapter 1, all employees have a duty of care to each other. This means we have:

✔ a duty to treat each other with dignity and respect

✔ a responsibility for paying attention to the effects of our actions on others

✔ a need for self-awareness and for seeking feedback

✔ an obligation to correct behaviour that causes offence or harm

UK employment law makes explicit this duty of care. If you think you may have been bullying people, take action now, without being prompted. It will be infinitely more comfortable and less expensive than the alternative of waiting until you are reported and sacked or brought to answer in court. Get help from your line manager or personnel department to improve the way you behave at work and you'll reap the reward of a clear conscience and better working relationships.

Accused of bullying? Alternative scenarios

Have you upset somebody by mistake?

✔ Apologise and change.

Do you feel that your behaviour should not have upset them?

✔ Express surprise.
✔ Explain that there was no intent to upset.
✔ Apologise for the upset caused.
✔ Ask what alternative behaviour would be more appropriate in their view. You don't have to agree, but this is a starting point for negotiating future behaviour patterns that are more comfortable for all concerned.

Are you accused of something that is untrue?

✓ Tell your line manager about the accusation and that you consider it untrue.

✓ If you are a union member, ask your union to help.

✓ Talk to your company's HR department, if it has one.

✓ Respond to the allegation, clearly stating which facts you believe to be accurate and your side of events where your view of events is different.

Step three: Take action as a manager or employer

Research conducted by the Chartered Institute of Personnel and Development (CIPD) has shown that most employers don't do enough to tackle the problem of bullying. As mentioned above, employers have a duty of care towards employees. If you are a manager and you don't respond to reports of bullying, your employees may bring a case against you for constructive dismissal. By not providing a safe working environment, you're breaching implied terms of contract. So what should employers do about bullying?

✓ Devise a bullying policy in consultation with staff and unions.

✓ Set a good example by training senior managers.

✔ Deal promptly and properly with complaints and reports of bullying.

✔ Communicate the policy and procedures.

✔ Encourage employees to come forward for help.

✔ Monitor and seek out bullying.

✔ Intervene early to restore a healthy culture in areas of the organisation where you suspect bullying may arise.

In surveys, the primary reason given for bullying happening at work is that 'the bullies do it because they can get away with it'. When organisations apply well thought-out anti-bullying policies, it becomes obvious to all that 'round here, we don't put up with bullying', and pretty soon the culture becomes healthier for all.

Common mistakes

✘ **Senior managers go into denial**

A recent CIPD survey of 1000 employers found that most admitted they did not do enough to tackle the problem. Acting against an organisation's bullies isn't work that a lot of people relish, and often senior managers may try to sweep it under the carpet in the hope that it will go away.

Some of them may even hold mistaken beliefs, such as:

■ **There isn't any bullying taking place here!**

In fact, research shows bullying to be spread across *all* levels in all types of organisations. Uniformed services are particularly prone to it.

■ **It is not worth devoting resources to sorting it out.**

Really? It's very expensive:

- ■ to lose your reputation
- ■ to be taken to court
- ■ to have high staff turnover rates—22% of witnesses leave their jobs as a result of bullying
- ■ to have reduced productivity—targets report working at 85% of normal capacity, compared with 92% for employees not affected by bullying

■ **I can't confront, upset, or dismiss key staff.**

Bullying is very damaging at the individual, group, and organisational level. Not acting appropriately against a bully supports that person's bad behaviour. It increases staff turnover in the short term, and creates or supports a culture of bullying in the long term.

STEPS TO SUCCESS

✔ If you are a manager or employer, be brave enough to take action to stamp out bullying in the workplace. 'Doing nothing' about it is a much riskier strategy for the future.

✔ Protect your organisation by making sure that it devises and implements strong anti-bullying policies.

✔ Understand bullying properly and involve staff from all parts and levels of the organisation in the production of anti-bullying policies.

✔ If you are accused of bullying, think long and hard about your behaviour at work. Trying to dismiss inappropriate behaviour with 'It's just the way I am' won't help. Take the feedback on board, act on it, and change your ways.

✔ If a colleague is being bullied and asks you for help, offer them as much support as you feel able to and put them in touch with people who can help directly, whether inside or outside the organisation.

Useful links

Chartered Institute of Personnel and Development:
www.cipd.co.uk
Public Concern at Work:
helpline@pcaw.co.uk

Where to find more help

Bullying at Work: How to Confront and Overcome It
Andrea Adams
London: Virago, 1992
256pp ISBN 185381542X
Based on three years' research, this popular book offers advice and help for anyone affected by bullying in the workplace. It looks at the psychological roots of bullying, helping others to understand why it happens and how it can be avoided in future.

Bully in Sight: How to Predict, Resist, Challenge and Combat Workplace Bullying – Overcoming the Silence and Denial by Which Abuse Thrives
Tim Field
Didcot: Success Unlimited
384pp ISBN: 0952912104
This book is another well-regarded work which offers insight, help, and advice to those suffering from workplace harassment. According to the Guardian, the late Tim Field 'believed that bullying was the single most important social issue of the days, most important', and his passionate concern for those who are going through this trauma comes across strongly in this landmark publication.

Bullies, Tyrants, and Impossible People: How to Beat Them Without Joining Them
Ronald Shapiro et al
New York: Crown Business, 2005
208pp, ISBN 1400050111
As the title suggests, this book offers advice on how we can deal with difficult people without stooping to their level. The authors suggest using the 'NICE' method: Neutralise your emotions, Identify type, Control the encounter, and Explore options. Practical and effective, the book combines advice and help with illuminating case studies.